Thanks to everyone who supported me while writing this book.

My partner, Jennifer, who believes in me no matter what!

Special mention to all of my boys: Mike, Josh, Nathan, Kyle and Matt.

Go class of 2024 - The Academy and The Ivy's all the way!

The sky is NOT the limit, it's just a view!

Boost Your Personal HR Brand (and your organization) Through Thought Leadership

What is Thought Leadership?   2
    Thought Leadership in a Nutshell   2
    The Value of Thought Leadership   3

How Thought Leadership Can Benefit Your Business   3
    Expertise, Brand Recognition, and Trust   4
    Exposure   5
    Conversions   5

How to Become a Thought Leader   5
    Carve Out Your Niche   6
    Identify Your USP   6
    Challenge the Status Quo   7
    Don't Forget to Stay Human   7
    Start Producing Content   8

Thought Leadership Content   8
    Thought Leadership Platforms   8
    Achieving Authentic Thought Leadership With Content   9
    Best Practices for Thought Leadership Content   10

Thought Leadership Strategy   11
    Step 1: Defining Your Goals   11
    Step 2: Research Existing Thought Leadership   12
    Step 3: Identify Your Focus and Your Thought Leaders   12
    Step 4: Create the Content   13
    Step 5: Publish and Promote Your Content   15

Give Thought Leadership a Try   17

What Is Thought Leadership?

If you're an HR team member or leader, you may not have considered thought leadership as a relevant strategy for your business. Generally, thought leaders quoted in the mainstream media tend to be associated with globally-recognized brands.

However, thought leaders can come from any business, big or small, in any industry. If you can provide value to your audience through information and education, you have the ability to be an effective thought leader. Most of the time, HR is at the forefront of getting information out to audience., so you may as well maximize your influence.

Thought Leadership in a Nutshell

A thought leader is seen as the authority on any given subject. He or she is the go-to person within a specific niche, like HR. Their opinions are trusted because they are the authority. They inspire others with innovative ideas and provide the guidance to turn ideas into reality.

Because of their expertise, thought leaders are respected by both peers and competitors. Their followers value and trust the thought leader's opinions to the degree that they incorporate those opinions into their lives.

Because they are so respected and such importance is given to their opinions and advice, thought leaders are often sought out to speak at conferences, do media interviews and write for publications relevant to their industry.

Business leaders aspire to become thought leaders within their field - an endeavor which takes patience, strategy and education. Most thought leaders are passionate about their subject area and enthusiastically share their knowledge with others.

Thought leadership requires insight and innovative thinking. By utilizing content marketing, social media, and other communication methods, you can increase your authority within your company, and influence the trends and direction of your niche.

The Value of Thought Leadership

Thought leadership is an incredibly valuable marketing asset for your business. By becoming an HR thought leader within your industry, you build brand credibility and raise your profile as the best choice within your market.

So, if you're in a competitive market, becoming a thought leader can give you the edge when it comes time to convert applicants into an audience.

However, becoming an HR thought leader is not primarily just about marketing to candidates and hiring. It's about giving your audience and followers- oftentimes other HR colleagues - valuable and helpful information regarding specific topics within your industry.

Expertise, insight and a valuable perspective are the elements needed to be an effective thought leader.

Becoming a thought leader:

- Establishes your credibility within your company and industry
- Boosts your professional brand value and builds your industry presence
- Establishes you as an expert resource who can influence others within your industry
- Highlights your strengths
- Inspires forward-thinking in others

The goal of thought leadership is to build relationships based on your expert knowledge of your department, market or industry. When people are ready to make a career move, or want to make organizational changes, you offer, you will be at the top of their mind.

How Thought Leadership Can Benefit Your Business

When you consider thought leadership as a marketing strategy and incorporate it into your content you increase the credibility and authority of your brand.

When you have valuable information or ideas to pass along to your audience, it increases your prominence within your industry. As your profile increases, so does your audience which allows you to become an authority within your market.

Thought leadership allows you to push ideas that you want your audience to believe, which drives change in their perspective and creates trends.

Thought leadership also increases the chances that your audience will share and link back to your content which will strengthen your SEO. But beware - publishing content for thought leadership only to increase your audience or promote sharing can lessen the impact of your content. Your content should always be original, unique opinions based on your own research.

Content published for thought leadership is not intended to directly promote conversions. **However, it will help to build relationships with your audience and build professional brand awareness, which are part of the first stage in the marketing funnel.**

Expertise, Brand Recognition and Trust

Sharing industry expertise with your intended audience is the cornerstone of thought leadership. With so much information available today, people are looking for experts to help them separate fact from fiction.

When you put in the work to become a thought leader, you establish yourself as an expert and authority in your particular niche. By gaining the trust of your audience through your content, you create listeners that are willing to trust the information you provide to make decisions about their own lives, health and happiness.

Thought leadership is integral to helping your brand grow and reaching your audience. Additionally, it allows you to stay apprised of the trends driving your market.

The bottom line is that thought leadership content conveys your expertise within your industry to your audience. When your content is valuable and helps a person to solve a problem or addresses a real need in their life, it builds trust. When it comes time to take action, the brand recognition and trust you've established will pave the way for conversions.

In your market, what's going to differentiate you from your competition? The expertise you share with your audience can be the difference between a sale for you or a sale for the competition. The insights you offer to your customers through thought leadership will be highly valued and have a great influence over their decision to do business with you.

Exposure

As you build your reputation as an HR thought leader, your brand (and organization) will gain more exposure. This can come through the media, word-of-mouth from people following you, public speaking and more.

Thought leadership keeps you on the radar of the customers within the buying cycle. **More exposure means more brand awareness, which will help you when the time comes for the lead to convert.**

Thought leadership is not an SEO strategy per se, but if you do it right, it can lead to more people linking to your content which will strengthen your SEO. Stronger SEO leads to better ranking which leads to more organic search traffic to your content which grows your audience.

Conversions

Really, the goal of any marketing strategy that you implement is conversions. Thought leadership pulls your audience through a complete cycle of the sales funnel. From awareness to conversion, your thought leadership content can be there to keep building trust and nurturing them to the sale.

How to Become a Thought Leader

HR thought leaders have informed opinions about subjects within their industries of expertise. In order to be recognized as a thought leader, you need to have a proven track record you can show to others so they're confident you're a voice worth listening to.

It's going to take more than a LinkedIn profile to become a thought leader. It takes time, tenacity and talent to build your reputation. Start by researching, learning and developing your expertise within your current industry. Write content and put it on your blog and social media platforms. Build a following and begin the process of proving yourself as an expert in your field.

Thought leadership is about more than just knowledge. In order to be successful, you have to develop a rapport with your audience. You must share your knowledge, build trust and have a genuine desire to help your audience. When you do this, people can't help but be drawn in.

Carve Out Your Niche

Thought leaders are experts, but not in everything. No one can know everything. In order to be effective, it's best to demonstrate your expertise in a couple of key areas. Be careful to not stretch yourself too thin trying to cover everything - especially in HR!

You have to define your niche. The niche you choose should be relevant to your industry, experience and target audience.

Passion is an important aspect of choosing your niche, so it should be a consideration. You'll also want to choose an area that you already have significant expertise in, so that you are authentic.

If you lack expertise or passion, your message will fall flat and your goal of becoming a thought leader will be much more difficult.

Identify Your USP

Defining your USP, or Unique Selling Proposition is an important part of becoming a thought leader. Being able to pinpoint what makes you stand out gives your content direction and allows you to target your marketing successfully.

There are already many thought leaders in the world. Once you've identified your niche within the HR realm, you will need to define your USP.

If you are in HR, try analyzing what you "sell", not just the service characteristics of HR in general. Are you specializing in anything? Are you the compensation and payroll specialist? Do you specialize in benefits or engagement? Charles Revson, the founder of Revlon, always said he sold hope, not makeup. Neiman Marcus sells luxury, while Wal-Mart sells bargains. What is it you specialize in "selling?"

Let's dive into some helpful strategies for developing your USP.

- **Use the audience's(customer's) point of view.** Sometimes, we get so wrapped up in our own services that we forget that it's the customer that we have to make happy. Take a step back and consider what the customer wants and what problems they are trying to solve.

- **Know what motivates your audience.** Push yourself to go beyond traditional demographics and find out their motives. Also, ask yourself, "What is trending in the HR world right now and how can I contribute?"

- **Why will your (audience) customers believe you over someone else?** Figure out what qualities or characteristics your view of things have that can drive the conversation. Conversely, figure out the same for any competitor.

Once you've gone through this process, you need to clear out any preconceived ideas you have about your service and be very honest as you **answer these questions:**

- What **features** set you apart?
- What idea can you **promote** that will convert visitors?
- How can you **position yourself** to highlight your USP?

Challenge the Status Quo

Disrupt typical HR thinking and challenge the status quo. People are interested in new ideas, new ways of thinking and different points of view. You want your brand to be considered forward-thinking but not controversial just for the sake of being controversial. Don't lose your authenticity. Stay true to your message.

Challenging the status quo doesn't always mean that something needs to change. Sometimes, it can just be about proposing a new idea worth exploring. Even good things can be made great.

Thought leaders should have a forward thinking, growth mindset. Don't settle for the minimums. Look for the big ideas and expand on them.

Don't Forget to Stay Human - after all it is a part of our jobs!

A big part of HR thought leadership is humanizing your brand. You can accomplish this by sharing your story. Talk about your passion and motivation, but don't be afraid to be vulnerable as well. Sharing your challenges and weaknesses will tremendously impact your audience.

As a thought leader, you can identify with the challenges faced by your audience and then offer them strategies and solutions to overcome them. Be the human voice in HR always. We are HUMAN Resources.

Thought Leadership Content

Not everyone will become a thought leader and there are already lots of thought leaders out there. Being an HR thought leader doesn't necessarily mean you will become a household name but you will still gain a lot by becoming an authority in your industry.

Content marketing is an integral part of thought leadership. This is how you establish yourself as a thought leader within your industry and attract more leads to your business.

Thought Leadership Platforms

Content marketing can be done through many different channels.

Start publishing a blog. Launching a blog is a great starting point for finding and developing your thought leadership voice. As the author of your blog content, you are free to explore ideas, share your opinions and engage your audience with no restrictions.

This is a great way to find out what your audience is struggling with so you can present solutions. This is how you catapult yourself to the status of an industry leader.

Use social media to engage your followers even more. Don't forget to use your social media channels to promote your blog as well as engage your followers.

LinkedIn is an important platform for thought leadership. LinkedIn has over 600 million users worldwide. Utilize this site to network with others in your industry, gain brand recognition, and share your expertise by posting articles and opinion pieces.

It's important to optimize your profile. Be sure to include all of your relevant experience, skills and qualifications. Doing this will show others that you have the skills to back up your thoughts and what you have to say is worth listening to.

You can utilize LinkedIn groups to start discussions with others in your industry, as well as contribute to existing conversations and answer questions and concerns from other users.

Remember, **LinkedIn was created for networking.** When you actively share your knowledge and engage with other users you will be able to make connections and earn followers.

Podcasts can also be very helpful in building thought leadership. Either by being a guest on an existing podcast or starting your own, you can use a podcast to get your expertise and opinions out there, stay current on trends within your industry and invite others within your industry to share their thoughts.

Achieving Authentic Thought Leadership With Content

Engaging with people on a human level is the key to achieving authentic thought leadership, and actually should be a main component for Human Resources in general. Building your credibility as an HR thought leader through your content strategy creates an authentic, engaged audience for your business.

Here are five ways to achieve authenticity in your thought leadership strategy.

1. Start writing. Producing quality, value-driven content is one of the most effective ways to build thought leadership. It's also a great way to connect with and engage your audience. There are a lot of great ways to expose your target audience to your thoughts and opinions.

- **Start blogging:** Create your own blog for sure and publish new content consistently. You can also guest blog other reputable sites within your niche. The important thing is to establish your unique voice that displays your brand and expertise.

- **Publish your posts on platforms relevant to your industry:** Getting your work published where new audiences will be exposed to it is an important way to not only get your expertise recognized, but to also expand your own audience.

- **Post on social media:** Again, this is a great place to promote what you've written and drive more traffic to it.

2. Reach out to mentors and influencers. Partnering with mentors and influencers is a great way to expand your reach because they already have an established connection with their audience. Often, they already have a good amount of followers who respect their opinions and seek their advice when making decisions. They represent new marketing channels and ways of gaining exposure.

Locate influencers within human resources and follow them on different social media platforms. Comment on their posts and try to provide fresh perspectives and relevant insights. Engaging in this way lets you build a relationship with the influencer *and* their followers.

You can also try to build a relationship with the influencer by offering your assistance with a campaign or offering to contribute an article for their blog. Start this for free and build your reputation quickly.

3. Awards and accolades. Having a solid professional background in HR and verifiable experience is a solid foundation for building authority in any industry. Awards, credentials and honors can help you build credibility with your audience.

Building a platform that helps you to show your expertise, enhance your message and create new opportunities is the goal here. When you create an impressive platform, it's easier to draw a following, get speaking engagements and connect with a broad audience.

4. Leverage content marketing. Content marketing is a very effective way to educate, inform and increase your reach. Blog posts, relevant publications, infographics, ebooks, webinars, and videos are all ways to increase your organic traffic and broaden your audience.

An effective content marketing strategy starts with clear goals to reach your target market, position your brand and achieve your objectives.

Keep in mind that the purpose behind your content is not to market your company or its services. Your objective is to persuade readers or consumers that *you* and *your* professional brand are the authority within HR.

5. Engage your followers on social media. Billions of people worldwide are using social media. You can use it to broadcast your thought leadership and grow your audience. Using social media helps you to connect with more people and allows for easy engagement.

Share articles, post relevant thoughts and promote your blog posts. You can also consider going live to reach your audience instantly and authentically. Just remain mindful of staying on topic.

Best Practices for Thought Leadership Content

If you really want to utilize your content to its fullest potential, you can follow these tips when crafting your content.

- **Only publish high-quality content:** Quality is one of the most important aspects of thought leadership content. Low-quality content is not going to keep people engaged. Your content should always provide value to the person reading it. Stay mindful of your audience!

- **Don't over-promote:** If your goal is to become a thought leader in your industry, promoting your company's products and services is not your primary goal. Concentrate on the HR issue and solve your audience's problems within it.

- **Consistency is key:** Building trust with your audience doesn't happen with your first blog post. It takes time and publishing useful content on a consistent basis. Stay patient and consistent.

  Create a calendar so you have a direction for your content and then post regularly.

Authentic thought leaders are not just trying to earn a buck - they care about their industry and are passionate about helping others succeed.

- **Social media matters:** Complete your profiles on different channels and grow your following on social media. This is a great way to engage with your audience.

- **Remember, you're the expert:** High-quality, non-promotional content will showcase your brand and endear you to your audience as a thought leader.

Dedication to becoming an HR thought leader will humanize your brand and build trusting relationships with your audience. Share your insights, start conversations and reach out to other people in the HR world to make worthwhile connections. Remember, keep the human aspect in HR.

Thought Leadership Strategy

Developing a thought leadership strategy is not a one-size-fits-all type of deal. Many elements are the same for every industry while others will depend on the specifics of your speciality within HR. These strategies can be used even if you are not in HR!

Step 1: Define Your Goals

As with any strategy, your first step is to determine what you want to accomplish with your actions.

Consider how thought leadership can help you to achieve each of your existing goals. For example, if your goal is to broaden your brand recognition, you may develop content about problems HR within your industry - your target audience - is facing, and solutions that your ideas can offer.

Defining Your Target audience

It's always helpful, when considering your marketing goals, to know exactly who your audience is. Some well-developed buyer personas can help you with this but also consider others beyond those personas who might benefit from what you have to say.

Your audience doesn't necessarily correlate to only HR people. Thought leadership may go well beyond just those who are in HR. In thought leadership, you want to reach a more diverse audience - people who will talk about your brand, become part of the community you create and act as advocates for your branding.

Step 2: Research Existing Thought Leadership

After you've defined your goals and audience, it's time to do some research to discover the existing thought leadership within your HR niche. Check out different communication channels within your industry.

- Online and print trade publications, journals and newsletters
- Reputable news resources
- Online forums
- Brand platforms like LinkedIn and Medium
- Industry blogs
- Social media

- Webinars, conferences and seminars

As you conduct this research, pay close attention to what the existing thought leadership ideas and trends are. This will help you to understand the issues within your industry as well as familiarize yourself with who the current, primary thought leaders are.

Also, take note of what other thought leaders are addressing with their content. What trends do they see and how are they delivering their content? Keep the competition in mind while you develop your own thought leadership content.

Review your existing blog posts and communications to get a handle on what your position has previously been on topics within your industry. You don't want to make a huge shift or come across as controversial because you're contradicting a previously held position.

Step 3: Identify Your Focus

Step 3 is a bit more broad in scope. This is from the view of an HR person becoming or having a thought leader within an organization. In many companies, upper management and CEOs are the primary creators of thought leadership content. Other companies have SMEs (subject matter experts) create their content while others give this task to staff or freelance copywriters.

As you start identifying who your company's thought leaders are (or if you will represent your company in this area), there are a couple of things to consider.

- Before you even begin creating content, you have to understand on an organizational level where your thought leadership lies. What is your expertise? What do you specialize in?
- Then, spread out and consider your brand story and values. What changes do you want to make as a company? What changes would you like to see within your industry?

For your thought leadership to be effective, you and your thought leaders have to be authentic, independent thinkers. There are likely several topics of thought leadership that you'd like to speak on, so it's a good idea to develop a solid group of people who are going to be creating it.

As you consider the experts working within your organization, keep these things in mind:

- **Align your brand and values with your thought leadership.** If your thought leaders don't stand firmly behind your brand and its values, your story, and your position, your content is unlikely to have the desired effect within the organization. As mentioned before, know your audience.

- **Knowledge and expertise are key but don't forget passion.** Being knowledgeable and passionate about the subject matter will organically make others want to follow you.
- **Don't be afraid of revolutionary opinions and inspired ideas.** You will always run the risk of alienating some with your beliefs and you have to be okay with that. When it comes to thought leadership, you can't appeal to everyone. Be sure to use your brand story and values as guidelines for your content and know your audience.
- **Create great content.** This can include writing and speaking, being a guest on a podcast, hosting a webinar or event, etc. It's also helpful for thought leaders to have credentials or memberships from relevant organizations to help boost their credibility.

It's important that thought leadership comes directly from the experts in your organization, even if that isn't you. Leveraging your subject matter experts will help you to have the most helpful, relevant content. After all, these are the people who are in the trenches, solving the problems of your customers.

Give your SME content creators the byline on your content - this will help your reach as the SME shares the content with their audience.

Step 4: Create the Content

Now it's time to actually start creating content.

Research

A good starting point for creating thought leadership content is to simply take your knowledge of your goals and audience and then use this information to generate content ideas.

An important part of this process is to know what the current trends and topics are within your industry. This allows you to know what issues your audience is interested in so your content is received and consumed successfully.

By utilizing specialty tools, like topic research tools, you can quickly and efficiently determine trending topics. Choosing trending content topics for chosen keywords can give you a tremendous array of content ideas.

In addition to research and trending keywords, you can try these other ideas for finding solid thought leadership content ideas:

- **SME experience.** If you or your team have developed a unique or different way to solve a problem within your industry or have a great case study, use it as content. Just be sure not to use anything that may be proprietary.

- **Data and statistics.** If you have data or statistics that you have acquired due to the nature of your business, you can share that with others in your industry. This data could come from your customers, product, or research.

- **Unique opinions.** If your business embraces an opinion or thought process that goes against industry norms, share it with your audience. Use your brand story to ground the information.

- **Industry insights.** Have your experts share their opinions and/or expertise and use your company's data to back them up.

- **Collaborate.** Use your customers and industry partners to co-create content. You can also partner up with existing thought leaders and influencers within your industry.

- **Use your story.** People love reading or hearing about personal stories of success, failure, and the adventures along the way.

Creating a content calendar can really help your team collaborate on their content ideas to keep things from getting redundant.

Types of Thought Leadership Content

You briefly learned about thought leadership content in a previous chapter, but here we will dive into a little more detail.

Thought leadership content, as with most content, can come in any shape or form. According to research done by Semrush, a search engine marketing firm, here are the most popular types of thought leadership content being created.

• Articles/blog posts 91.4%	• Research 33.2%
• Video 44.1%	• Ebooks 29.9%
• Webinars/events 36.2%	• Podcasts 21.7%
• White papers 33.2%	• Data visualizations 20.7%

This research showed that articles and blog posts are by far the most popular thought leadership content format, at 91.4%. As you begin to start actually producing your thought leadership content, you'll want to consider a couple of things.

- **How will the content be produced?** As you begin to build your content calendar and assign topics, you need to determine who is actually going to be producing the content. Some of your experts will be really good writers and others will have great public speaking chops. Enlist them if this isn't your strong suite, and put them where they can let their strengths shine.

If your content will be written and your thought leader experts are not necessarily great writers, don't be afraid to connect with a professional copywriter. How the articles are written can have a substantial impact on the traffic and audience they attract.

- **Authenticity is imperative.** Remember, your content should be created in the spirit of a genuine desire to help others. Whether that be customers, colleagues, or others within your industry.

  Thought leadership content is not the time to boast about your company or try to sell your products or services. The best content is that which shares what you've learned or gives insight into how the reader can improve something to make their professional life better or make them more successful.

- **Be flexible.** Industry trends change quickly sometimes and since that is closely tied with thought leadership, you need to be prepared to switch things up accordingly.

Thought leadership is about creating value, sharing knowledge and creating revolutionary ideas. Small businesses and startups have the same opportunities in thought leadership as bigger, more well-known companies. You can make an impact whether you're a multi-million dollar company or just getting started. This works for B2B models as well as B2C.

Step 5: Publish and Promote Your Content

In order to have a successful thought leadership campaign, your content has to be consumed by your audience. If no one sees or hears what you have to say, there is no path forward. Distribution and promotion of your content is vital.

As mentioned above, you may have thought leaders on your team who can promote your content through their own networks. Promoting content on your channels, like blogs and social media is also an effective mode of promotion.

You could also consider pitching your content to journalists and publications within your industry, as well as influencers within your industry. Since thought leadership content tends to be more authentic and opinion-based, it can generate a lot of interest and attention.

If you are a small business or just getting started, you may find it more difficult to get the exposure you need to grow your audience with your thought leadership. If this is the case for you, there are several tactics you can try to get your content seen.

- **Try collaborations with other brands within your industry that aren't your competition.** Joint thought leadership content can help you form an alliance with another company with a similar agenda to yours.

- Consider asking for quotes and/or interviews from other relevant opinion leaders and influencers. They will tend to want to share the content with their audience, which could give you a boost.

- You can try using a service like Help a Reporter to pitch your content to journalists or offer your expertise on a piece they are working on.

- **Check out what is being published by other content creators within your industry and create similar, relevant content.** If you reach out to them, they may be willing to share your content with their audience.

- If you have the resources, you can try adding advertising to your strategy. A few strategically placed PPC ads on social media can bring a lot of relevant traffic.

Don't forget the importance of engagement. Thought leadership, at its core, is about starting conversations. Be sure to follow through and interact with the comments, communities and influencers that are discussing your content. Stay in touch and stay engaged with your audience. HR is ever changing and developing and your ideas are worth sharing!

Try using a brand monitoring tool so you can track when your brand is being discussed so you can reach out to those who are interested in what you have to say.

Give Thought Leadership a Try

As you can see, thought leadership can be a powerful strategy for you as an HR practitioner, and also for your organization. When you become an expert and build trusting relationships with your audience, you can create powerful professional gains.

Here are the steps again:
1. Define your goals
2. Research existing thought leadership
3. Identify your focus
4. Create the content
5. Publish and promote your content, and
6. GO DO IT!

Think about this; One of the most prolific thought leaders in modern times was Steve Jobs. He believed that you had to be a *little different* to buy an Apple computer. This is where the 'Think Different' ad campaign was born. It featured real geniuses whose *crazy* ideas had a profound impact on the world. That's exactly what thought leadership is all about.

Now get out there and be a thought leader inside HR and out. As a thought leader, go change HR for the better!

Good Luck!

-Sonya

Use the following pages to jot down notes on some topics that you could develop into your own topics

Jot down notes on some topics that you could develop into your own leadership thoughts

Jot down notes on some topics that you could develop into your own leadership thoughts

Jot down notes on some topics that you could develop into your own leadership thoughts

www.ingramcontent.com/pod-product-compliance
Lightning Source LLC
Chambersburg PA
CBHW071002220526
45471CB00007B/3141